The Stepkin Stories

Helping Children Cope with Divorce and Adjust to Stepfamilies

Peggy Lumpkin

BookPartners
Wilsonville, Oregon

Cover design by Richard Ferguson
Text design by Sheryl Mehary

BookPartners, Inc.
P.O. Box 922
Wilsonville, Oregon 97070

This book is dedicated to you, the caring adult who is helping a child successfully adapt to the many challenges of divorce and stepfamilies. May your positive efforts blossom in an emotionally healthy child.

Acknowledgments

A complete list of all the people who helped me along the way with this book would be another book in itself. Countless contributions, large and small, came from teachers, parents, librarians, friends, psychologists, psychiatrists, counselors, and social workers who recognize the need to help the millions of children who experience divorce in their families. By virtue of simply being adults, we are all collectively responsible for the welfare of all children.

I would also like to give special thanks to the children, especially my own, Mario and Dei, who helped create the Stepkin characters as wise and whimsical little people living under the steps. And lastly I give thanks to my husband, Dale, and everyone at BookPartners whose talents and guidance have made the dream of this book become a reality.

Contents

Introduction and General Instructions

The Stepkin Stories are designed for young children and are to be read by a parent, teacher, counselor, therapist, grandparent, librarian, or any other concerned adult. Each of the stories covers a particular aspect of divorce and can be read aloud in approximately ten minutes.

- **The Great Stepkin Mystery** is designed to help children deal with the initial problems of a divorce.
- **Stepkins to the Rescue** covers some sensitive problems that develop when a parent starts to date.
- **Moochie Finds a Stepkin** helps the child whose parent remarries.
- **Stepkin Holidays** shows the child how to relate to a stepparent.
- **Jamie and the Stepkins** covers problems typically encountered between stepsiblings.
- **Sailing with the Stepkins** helps the relationship between the child and the noncustodial stepfamily.
- **Stepkin Summer** helps children cope while visiting stepfamilies.

Stepkins are small fantasy people whom children discover living under steps. Unlike those nasty step relatives in classic fairy tales, the Stepkins provide a positive association when children hear the word "step."

The intent of *The Stepkin Stories* is to offer enough adventure and fantasy to hold the attention of a young child, while gently conveying valuable information about how to cope with the many difficult issues of divorce. Fantasy characters make learning the facts the children need to know about divorce less threatening.

< 1 >

Using the Guides

At the beginning of each story, you will find a description of some negative reactions caused by the particular aspect of divorce or stepfamilies being discussed in the story. Some of the most common responses seen in children are used in more than one story.

Children may show any combination of these reactions at different times. The child's age will have a major effect on which reactions he or she experiences.

Children **under two years old** may show signs of increased general anxiety, irritability, or sullenness.

Children **between the ages of three and five years** most often experience guilt feelings, denial, low self-esteem, regression, increased aggression, or pervasive neediness.

Children **between the ages of six and eight** more commonly show anger, fear, sadness, and rejection, or they may feel betrayed or repress their feelings.

As you read (or after you read) a story to the child, you can use the questions suggested in the illustrations to help the child discuss the reactions of the characters in the stories. For example: After you ask the suggested question, "Why is Kelly feeling so sad?" you can ask, "Have you ever felt like Kelly?" or "Do you know anyone who feels like Kelly?" You should adjust your discussion to the age level of the child.

Do not be discouraged if the child is not ready to talk right away. If you continue to explain the ideas in the guides, the child can gradually move toward understanding and coping with the situation.

The guides suggest specific ideas for the adult to emphasize with the child to make the child's adjustment to the divorce or stepfamily easier. The prevalence of divorce today makes this information also valuable for children whose parents are not divorced but who have friends going through these situations or who worry about divorce as a possibility in their own family. The end of a relationship involving two unmarried adults may cause the same reactions in the children as a divorce.

< 2 >

This book is intended as an aid to help children cope with divorce and stepfamilies by seeing how story children cope in similar predicaments. It does not claim to be an instant remedy for grief and anger caused by divorce.

We strongly recommend the help of a counselor, psychologist, or member of the clergy if at all possible. There may be no other time during childhood when professionals can be of more value than when the child is dealing with a divorce or stepfamilies.

Your local library can be an excellent source of information about support groups, non-profit organizations, and reference books dealing with divorce and stepfamilies.

< 3 >

The Great Stepkin Mystery

A story of a child's initial reaction to her parents' divorce and how she begins to cope.

< 5 >

The Great Stepkin Mystery

Before beginning this story, see general instructions on page 1.

In this story, a young girl named Kelly Smithers exhibits several common reactions to her parents' divorce. You may observe some or all of these reactions in the child you are helping:

Fear of Abandonment: Feelings of anxiety often result because the child has seen the dissolution of the parents' relationship and feels his/her own relationship with the parents is also in jeopardy.

Guilt Feelings: Young children frequently take the responsibility for the divorce on their own shoulders. They think that if they had not acted badly, the divorce would not have happened. This sense of control also leads them to believe it is their duty to reconcile the parents and restore the marriage.

Denial: The denial phase often occurs in divorce the same way it does with a death or other tragic loss. The child must move through this phase to acceptance before he/she can address the changes caused by the divorce.

Withdrawal: The common stress reaction of seeking isolation is a form of avoidance. In children, this may include alienation from friends, refusal to go to school or day care, or refusal to stay with a babysitter.

Regression: A child may subconsciously revert to babylike habits in an attempt both to recapture a happier time in the past and to obtain more attention from parents who are frequently preoccupied with their own problems during the divorce.

Reconciliation Fantasy: Children will not only often spend time fantasizing about the family being restored, but they will sometimes feel their wishful thinking can actually make things return to the way they once were.

< 6 >

Reading this story to the child will help him/her realize these feelings are normal in a divorce situation. If you then discuss Kelly's problems and how she learns to cope with them, you can gradually begin to talk with the child about his or her own feelings and reactions to the divorce.

Using your own words and examples, explain the following points to the child:

- Even though the parents are separating, the child is not being abandoned. Children will always be taken care of.
- Parents do not divorce to hurt or punish the child, though children often feel the divorce is directed toward them.
- The child did not cause the divorce. Parents do not divorce because children are bad.
- Children need to talk about their feelings and actively find ways to work things out. It is normal to feel anger, sadness, fear, shame, or confusion.
- The form of the family relationship will change with the divorce, but the parent-child relationship is not lost. Parents are co-parents, though they are not together.
- Children can be happier in a divorced home than in one where the parents are angry, fighting, or unhappy. Sometimes it is better for the parents not to live together.
- Sometimes other adults will be involved in the decision about the child's living arrangements, such as lawyers, judges, and family counselors.
- Wishful thinking on the child's part will not bring the parents back together again.

< 7 >

Why is Kelly feeling so sad?

< 8 >

Kelly Smithers ran out of the house as fast as she could. She couldn't stand to hear Mommy shouting on the phone, especially when Kelly knew Daddy was on the other end shouting right back.

She wanted this fighting to stop.

Kelly felt so gloomy as she sat on the porch steps with her best friend—her special blanket. She snuggled it close to her ear and stuck her favorite thumb in her mouth.

Kelly hoped no one would see, because everyone told her she was too old for such baby things as a security blanket and sucking her thumb. But this was a special emergency.

Kelly hated it so much when Mommy and Daddy got mad at each other. Didn't they know they were supposed to be a happy family?

But what was this she heard?

Oh, no! It was Mommy crying again.

Kelly ran inside to help, dropping her blanket on the porch.

"Mommy, Mommy—please don't cry," Kelly said. "Daddy will be back soon."

Mommy wiped her tears away with her apron. "Now, Kelly," Mommy explained about the divorce, "Daddy won't be coming back home. Remember? You'll go to visit him sometimes."

"But, Mommy..." Kelly tried to keep from breaking into tears herself.

Kelly had been hoping to get Mommy and Daddy together again, so she had been telling her friends her daddy was on a long trip. She was certain Daddy would come back some day because she was wishing for it harder than she had ever wished for anything in her life. She hadn't even wished that hard for her bride doll. And, after all, she got the doll, didn't she?

< 9 >

Why does Kelly want her special blanket?

< 10 >

But so far, her wishing hadn't helped Mommy and Daddy get back together. And now Kelly felt less and less like playing with her friends whose families were together. Sometimes she said she was sick so she would not have to go to school. Kelly just didn't feel like doing much of anything.

It was no use fighting back the tears, so Kelly ran outside again to get her special blanket. Maybe a juicy thumb and her blanket would make her feel better.

But when she looked on the porch where she was sure she had left it, her blanket was nowhere to be found.

Where could it be?

Who could have taken it?

Could it have fallen down the stairs?

Could the wind have blown it away?

Kelly began to search around the porch. She checked in the mail slot. She checked in the milk box. She even checked under the pot of flowers.

But her blanket was nowhere to be seen. Kelly thought it must have fallen under the steps, so down she climbed to wiggle underneath the stairs.

"This is very strange," she thought. "Why is it so bright under these dark steps?"

Then her eyes opened very wide when she realized there was a pair of eyes staring right back at her.

She blinked at them.

They blinked at her.

And then she blinked again, because she could not believe what she saw.

< 11 >

Why did Kelly pretend her daddy was on a trip?

< 12 >

There, under the stairs, was a tiny girl, no taller than a step. She looked so pretty, so sweet, and so small.

The loveliest thing about her was a pair of twinkling lights that came out from just above her ears.

Kelly might have been afraid, except for the friendly smile on the little one's face.

"Hello," she said nervously, "My name is Kelly Smithers. Can you talk?"

"Of course, and I can sing too. That's why my name is Melody," the tiny girl said. "Can you sing?"

"Well," said Kelly, remembering how terrible things were at home, "I used to sing when I was happy. But now I'm too sad."

"Sounds like you need some cheering up. I know. You can come and meet my mother," said Melody. "Her Honey-Butter Cookies can cheer up anyone. Momma is the best cookie baker of all the Stepkins."

"What are Stepkins?" Kelly asked.

"Stepkins are people who live under your stairs. We make sure the steps don't squeak or creak. Come and meet Momma."

So Kelly wiggled under the stairs to the little step home made from tossed-away treasures from the big world outside.

< 13 >

Can Kelly stop the divorce from happening?

< 14 >

For furniture there was a raisin-box sofa and a tin-can table.

Momma Stepkin was busy working on her sewing. She welcomed Kelly to her charming home, and from a matchbox cupboard, she took down bottle cap dishes to serve the girls her Honey-Butter Cookies.

"My new friend Kelly needs some cheering up, Momma," said Melody.

"Why are you so sad, Kelly?" asked Momma Stepkin.

Kelly tried to smile, but tears got in the way as she told her story to Melody and Momma Stepkin.

"I hate this fighting between Mommy and Daddy. I want my family back to normal again. This just doesn't feel right," she sobbed. "I'm trying my best to fix our family, but it hasn't worked so far."

Melody took out some cookies from the cookie jar, hoping they would help to cheer up Kelly.

"It's all right to cry, but let me ask you a question. If you could have your best wish, Kelly, how would things be?" asked Momma Stepkin.

"Well, I'd like Mommy and Daddy to be happy together," said Kelly.

"Are they happy when they're together?" asked Momma Stepkin.

"No, they told me they were sad being together, that's why they wanted a divorce," Kelly said.

"Now, if you had your choice," asked Momma, sitting down in a rocking chair, "would you rather have them together and sad, or happier with a divorce?"

Kelly looked down at the floor. "But maybe if I were really, really extra good, we could be a happy family."

< 15 >

What can Kelly do to make herself feel happier?

< 16 >

"You'll always be a family, Kelly," said Momma Stepkin. "But in a different way now. Your mother is still your mother, and your father is still your father. But now they are no longer husband and wife."

But my friends have parents who are married and happy," cried Kelly. "I don't want to tell them my parents are different."

"Friends want to help you when you're sad, Kelly. They don't need you to be just like them. Friends just want you to care about them and be honest. And if their parents get divorced, you can help each other. Now, how about another cookie?"

"But if there might be a chance I could fix things," said Kelly, "shouldn't I try?"

"No," said Momma. "Children cannot make decisions for their parents. You cannot cause a divorce. You cannot fix a marriage. Parents usually do not get married to each other again, but they can stay friends with each other."

"But how can I help them?" asked Kelly, nibbling her last cookie.

"Lots of hugs and kisses always help!" said Momma Stepkin.

That reminded Kelly how sad Mommy had been when Kelly left her. "I think Mommy needs some hugs and kisses right now."

"Well, do come back and visit us again," said Momma Stepkin as she returned to her sewing project. "I should have our lovely new curtains finished soon."

Momma Stepkin used a drinking straw for a curtain rod and began fastening her new curtains to it.

Suddenly, Kelly recognized the curtains. They were made from her own special blanket! So the mystery of her disappearing blanket was finally solved.

< 17 >

What can Kelly do to help her mom feel happier?

< 18 >

Seeing her blanket made Kelly want to snuggle it right away, but she didn't ask for it back. She thought to herself, "I'll go snuggle Mommy instead and let the Stepkins keep my blanket for their new curtains."

As Kelly left the little Stepkin home, Momma Stepkin said, "Kelly, it is okay for you to be afraid, or angry, or sad. But I'll tell you a secret. Everyone has a special helper inside who can make those feelings go away. It's not someone you can see with your eyes, so if you want to talk with your helper, just close your eyes and be very still for awhile. You can feel the helper as a beautiful bright light in your heart. If you ask to be happy, your helper will make you happier. If you ask your helper inside to make you brave, you will start to become brave. That special helper is always with you, and with your family, and with everyone, in every place."

That night, Mommy came to tuck Kelly into bed. When Daddy had been home, he always used to read Kelly a bedtime story. Kelly missed that more than anything.

"Mommy, would you read me a story?" asked Kelly. "Please."

Mommy smiled and reached for a storybook from the shelf. Then, she noticed something missing and said, "Kelly, where's your blanket, Honey?"

"Oh, that?" said Kelly. "Somebody else needed it more than I do."

Kelly was sleepy by the time Mommy finished reading.

"Wasn't that a happy ending?" she asked Kelly.

"Yes," said Kelly, yawning, "I guess there are lots of different ways to be happy."

Then Kelly closed her eyes and was very still. Soon she felt a warm light start to grow inside that let her know she could be happy too.

< 19 >

Stepkins
to the
Rescue

How children deal with problems encountered when a parent begins dating after a divorce.

< 21 >

Stepkins to the Rescue

Before beginning this story, see general instructions on page 1.

In this story, a sister and brother, Cassie and Alex Magoo, exhibit several common reactions when their custodial mother begins to date. You may have observed some or all of these reactions in the child you are helping:

Jealousy: Children often have very possessive feelings toward parents, especially those of the opposite sex. They sometimes perceive a parent's new companion as a threat to their own relationship with the parent.

Fear of Abandonment: Anxiety feelings often result because the child has seen the dissolution of the parents' relationship and feels his/her own relationship with the parent is also in jeopardy. Additionally, they often see a parent's new partner as another potential for loss of the new attachment.

Retaliation: Children frequently try to sabotage a parent's new relationship by acting out, regressing, or manipulating. Often they are expressing anger about the initial divorce.

Allegiance to the Absent Parent: Children may see a parent's new relationship as betrayal of the ex-spouse. Consequently, they feel guilty about showing affection to a parent's new partner and will show fierce loyalty toward the absent parent.

Reconciliation Fantasy: Children will not only often spend time fantasizing about the family being restored, but they will sometimes feel their wishful thinking can actually make things change the way they would like.

< 22 >

Reading this story with the child will help him/her realize these feelings are normal after a divorce when a parent starts dating. If you then discuss Cassie and Alex Magoo's problems and how they begin to cope with them, you can gradually begin to talk with the child about his or her own feelings and reactions.

Using your own words and examples, explain the following points to the child:

- Parents need the companionship of other adults in addition to children. Children cannot fill the place of an adult.
- Parents seldom remarry a former spouse, but they can continue a friendly relationship.
- The child's actions will not bring about a reconciliation of the parents.
- Establishing a relationship with a parent's new partner is not betrayal of the absent parent.
- The form of the family relationship has changed with the divorce, but the parent-child relationship is not lost. Parents are co-parents.
- Children need to talk about their feelings and actively find ways to work things out.
- The child does not have to like a parent's new friend, but he or she should be polite.

< 23 >

Why don't Cassie and Alex want their mother to go out on a date?

< 24 >

Cassie and Alex Magoo had a plan they were quite certain would stop their mother from dating. Even though it had been quite awhile since Mom and Dad's divorce, the children did not like the idea of their mother finding someone new.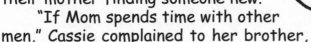

"If Mom spends time with other men," Cassie complained to her brother, "it will be harder to get her back together with Dad." Cassie was hoping that would happen some day.

"And she'll have less time to spend with us," agreed Alex. He wanted Mom to see that he could take care of her, even though he was still a young boy.

They had to work fast because that very night Mom was planning to go out to dinner with a man named Brett. But if Cassie and Alex had their way, Brett would leave before he even rang the door bell. They would fix it so he would never come back again.

First, they got Cassie's pet hamster, Chubby, and Alex's pet frog, Pug, and put them on the front porch. They put a sign on Chubby's cage that read "GEORGE GREEN, MAILMAN," and they put a sign on Pug's aquarium that said "FRED BROWN, MILKMAN." Then they found the empty cage that used to belong to their pet rat who had died last summer. They set the cage on the porch and put a sign on it that read "FOR BRETT."

They were going to make Brett believe their mother was really a witch who changed men into animals. That would scare him away for good.

< 25 >

Why are Cassie and Alex worried about sharing their mother with someone else?

< 26 >

Next, they took an old bucket and filled it with water and dirt and smashed leaves. They had never seen a witch's magic potion, but they thought it must look something like the mess they mixed up in the bucket. Then, to make things more believable, they took an old broom from the garage, and Alex glued on some wings from his old broken airplane model.

"This must be what a flying broom looks like," said Alex, proud of his work.

"And look," said Cassie, "I found the rubber spiders and bats we bought last Halloween. Do you think they look awful enough to scare Brett away?"

"One look at this place," smiled Alex, "and he'll think he's going to be the witch's next victim. We'll never hear from him again. And then we'll have Mom all to ourselves."

Alex climbed on the empty cage to hang the rubber spiders and bats from the top of the front door, but it was very hard to reach.

The cage wobbled and creaked, and then it suddenly crashed. Alex tumbled down with a thud! He landed so hard he fell through an old board in the porch, and the bucket of witch's potion fell on top of his head.

He didn't know where he was for a minute. Cassie poked her head down and asked, "Are you all right?"

< 27 >

Why does Cassie and Alex's mother need to spend time with other adults?

< 28 >

Alex blinked and stuttered, "I—I don't think so. I'm seeing things...like tiny people! And they look so real."

"We certainly are real," said one of the little ones, "as real as the hole you made in our ceiling."

"You nearly squashed me like a bug!" said the other one.

Cassie climbed down beside Alex when she heard the tiny voices. Alex wasn't imagining things at all. There, standing before Cassie and Alex, were two little people. One looked like a tiny boy, and one looked like a tiny girl. And they had beautiful twinkling lights above their ears.

"I'm Migsy," said the girl, "and this is my brother, Muggles."

"Why are you so small?" asked Cassie.

"Small!" scowled Muggles. "We're quite tall for Stepkins. We fit under the stairs just perfectly. At least, we did before you broke our roof."

Cassie said, "Boy, is Mom going to be mad when she sees what we did to the porch. And Brett will be here soon."

Alex just groaned and put his head in his hands.

< 29 >

Can Cassie and Alex care about Brett and their
father too?

< 30 >

"Who is Brett?" asked Muggles.

"Oh, he's this man Mom has been dating. And we've been trying to get him to stop coming to our house!" said Alex.

"Why?" asked Migsy. "Doesn't your mother like him?"

"Oh, sure," said Cassie. "But if she spends too much time with Brett, she won't have time for us."

"Is she happier when she gets to spend time with Brett?" asked Muggles.

"Well, yes. She says she needs some private time with adults once in awhile," said Cassie.

"So if you had the choice between spending lots of time with an unhappy mom, or less time with a happy mom, which would you choose?" asked Muggles.

Cassie and Alex looked at each other and both said, "Happy."

"But," Alex said, "we were hoping Mom and Dad would get back together again."

"Have they both said they wanted to?" asked Migsy, brushing some splinters out of Alex's hair.

"No," said Alex.

"Then it will probably not happen, because they have happier lives apart. So that's the way it should be," said Migsy.

"But we can take care of Mom without Brett," said Alex.

"Children cannot take care of adults," said Muggles.

"That's right," Migsy added while she began sweeping up the mess on the floor.

< 31 >

What can Cassie and Alex do for their mother?

< 32 >

"Don't worry if you don't like your mom's new friends right away. It may take time. You just have to be sure that you are always polite to them. That will make your mother proud of you," said Migsy.

"And be sure to tell her about your feelings," said Muggles, "so she can help you understand them."

"Well, we sure made a mess of things today," said Alex, looking up at the broken boards. "We're so sorry we wrecked your home. I guess we're going to be in big trouble."

Migsy and Muggles just smiled at each other.

"Don't worry," said Muggles. "We know how to take care of steps. Just watch."

Migsy and Muggles took out all the tools they would need for the repair job, tools tossed away and forgotten in the big world outside, found by the handy little Stepkins.

Tap, tap. Buzz, buzz. They hammered and they sawed. They measured and they trimmed. Before long, the broken porch was repaired. But it was even better than before because Migsy and Muggles had built a secret door for Cassie and Alex to use whenever they wanted to climb under the stairs.

"Now you can come and see us anytime you like," said Migsy.

"We'll knock on the secret door first, to see if you're home," said Alex. "But right now, we better clean up the porch before Brett comes."

They said good-bye to Migsy and Muggles and began to pick up the mess on the porch.

< 33 >

How does Brett show Cassie and Alex that he cares about them?

< 34 >

Suddenly, they heard a car drive up. Brett got out of his car and began walking toward the house.

"Hi," he said, greeting Cassie and Alex with a smile.

"Uh, uh...hi," they said, quickly trying to think up an excuse for why the porch looked so strange.

Noticing the mess, Brett said, "It looks like you two have been having a great time. Too bad having fun seems to make such a big mess. Why don't I help you clean it up before your mom sees it. You know how she likes things tidy."

< 35 >

How can Cassie and Alex help themselves feel
happier?

< 36 >

Whether or not Brett saw the cage with his name on it, the children never knew because he didn't say a word about it. But, what he did say was, "Nice looking frog and hamster you have here."

Alex said, "The frog is mine. My dad gave him to me."

"Oh. Your mom told me how good your dad is with animals," said Brett.

The children looked at each other, a bit surprised. They decided if it was all right for Mom to say something nice to Brett about Dad, then it must be okay for them, too.

"My father really loves animals," said Alex.

"I do, too," said Brett. "In fact, I have a dog named Brady. He's old, but he likes children. Maybe you two would like to come over and play with him sometime."

"Sure," said Cassie, remembering how much she and Alex used to love playing with their old dog, Rascal, who had died last year.

Brett said, "Shall we ask Mom if this Sunday is all right?"

Cassie and Alex's smiles went away. "That's our day to visit Dad," said Alex, hoping Brett wouldn't be upset.

Brett's smile never changed. "Well, what about Saturday then?"

"Great!" they said together and ran into the house to ask Mom, who was all set to go out on the date.

< 37 >

How can Cassie and Alex let their father know how they feel?

< 38 >

After Mom and Brett left, Cassie said to Alex, "Do you think Dad's feelings will be hurt if he knows we have fun with Brett?"

"Well," said Alex, "I think Dad is happier when we're happy, because he doesn't feel so guilty. If we make sure we show Dad that we love him, I don't think he'll mind about Brett."

"And the Stepkins said to be honest about our feelings, so I guess that means with Dad, too," said Cassie.

"I guess so," said Alex. "Hey, why don't we try out our new secret door on the porch?"

"Great idea!" said Cassie.

So Cassie and Alex ran to the front porch to visit their new friends. They wanted to thank Migsy and Muggles for rescuing them from what could have been a very big mistake.

< 39 >

Moochie
Finds a
Stepkin

A story of the problems facing a child when a parent remarries after a divorce.

< 41 >

Moochie Finds a Stepkin

Before beginning this story, see general instructions on page 1.

In this story, a young girl named Sadie Snodgrass exhibits several common reactions when her mother remarries. You may have observed some or all of these reactions in the child you are helping:

Withdrawal: The common stress reaction of seeking isolation is a form of avoidance. In children, this may include alienation from friends, refusal to go to school or day care, or refusal to stay with a baby sitter.

Anger: The remarriage of a parent often destroys the child's fantasy that the natural parents will someday reconcile. The result is anger toward the new stepparent and toward the parent who remarries.

Jealousy: Children often have very possessive feelings toward parents, especially those of the opposite sex. They sometimes perceive a parent's new spouse as a threat to their own relationship with the parent.

Retaliation: Children frequently try to sabotage a parent's new relationship by acting out, regressing, or manipulating. Often they are still expressing their anger about the initial divorce.

Allegiance to the Absent Parent: Children may see the remarriage of a parent as a betrayal of the ex-spouse. Consequently they feel guilty about showing affection toward a parent's new spouse and will show fierce loyalty toward the absent parent.

< 42 >

Reading this story with the child will help him/her realize these feelings are normal when a divorced parent remarries. If you then discuss Sadie's problems and how she begins to cope with them, you can gradually begin to talk with the child about his or her own feelings and reactions.

Using your own words and examples, explain the following points to the child:

- Establishing a relationship with a parent's new spouse is not a betrayal of the absent parent.
- The child may not love the new stepparent right away, but he or she does need to be polite and accept the authority of the stepparent as an adult.
- The relationship with the new stepparent will not be the same as with the absent parent. One relationship need not diminish the other.
- A parent's love for the child is no less because the parent remarries.
- Each child has a responsibility to be a contributor to the family and may need to become more independent.
- Children need to talk about their feelings and actively find ways to make things work.
- Parents show their love and caring by the things they do for other family members.

< 43 >

Why did Sadie want to be alone after her mother got married?

< 44 >

Poor Sadie Snodgrass was so lonely.

Thank goodness she had at least one friend—her dog, Moochie the Pooch.

Sadie's family had been changed around lately, and Sadie was mad about quite a few things.

It started when Dad left home. Sadie was not only mad at Dad for leaving, but she was also mad at Mom for not trying harder to make him stay. Sadie wished and wished he would come back. But no matter how hard she wished, it just didn't happen.

After awhile, Mom met a gentleman named Rudy, and they decided to get married. When Sadie heard the news, she felt strange, and she didn't want to spend time with anyone but Moochie.

"You're the only one who really loves me," Sadie said to Moochie. "And you love just me."

Sadie spent a lot of time with her arms around Moochie's neck, burying her head in his soft fur. She had quite a bit of time alone now, because Mom and Rudy went on a vacation after the wedding, their honeymoon. Auntie Peg had come to stay with Sadie.

"They didn't even invite me along," Sadie said to Moochie. "I guess they're going to be so busy with each other, no one will have time for me."

< 45 >

Why did Sadie try to make faces in the wedding pictures?

< 46 >

Sadie felt even worse because she had done something she wasn't very proud of. At Mom's wedding, the photographer tried to take pictures of the new family. But every time he said, "Smile, everyone," Sadie made the most horrible faces.

In one picture she stuck out her tongue. In another, she hid her face behind a flower basket. Sadie knew this had hurt Mom's feelings, but she just couldn't make herself smile about the wedding, because it ruined so many of her hopes about Mom and Dad.

But spoiling the pictures didn't help Sadie feel better at all. She just felt confused and naughty, especially since Rudy had just built a brand new doghouse for Moochie in the backyard.

So Sadie just moped around, thinking about how unlucky she was to be left home with Auntie Peg while Mom was on the honeymoon.

Auntie Peg said Sadie should go outside and play, instead of sitting around the house all day.

"Come on, Moochie," said Sadie. "Let's go see what's in the empty lot next door."

So the two began to slowly wander through the weeds and bushes next door. Suddenly Moochie stopped, growled, and then ran off into the bushes.

"Hey, come back here," Sadie yelled after Moochie. "Where do you think you're going?"

But Moochie paid no attention to her, and all she could hear was some rustling in the weeds. Then, she heard what sounded like a tiny scream.

"Help! Help! Help! It's a monster!" she heard a little voice say.

< 47 >

How did Rudy show that he cares about Sadie?

< 48 >

Then out stepped Moochie. His eyes shining brightly, he was holding the strangest thing in his mouth.

Squeaking and squealing, the tiny thing cried, "Please tell this beast to put me down."

Moochie brought it over to Sadie and she took a long, long look at the small, small thing.

At first, Sadie thought it was someone's lost doll, but soon she realized it was a tiny girl with beautiful twinkling lights coming out of her hair. She looked so frightened that Sadie yelled, "Put her down, Moochie."

Safely on the ground, the tiny girl said, "Oh, thank you for saving me from the monster."

"But, he's not a monster," said Sadie. "He's my dog, Moochie the Pooch. And I'm Sadie Snodgrass. Moochie would never hurt anyone at all. It's just that we've never seen anything so special as you before."

The little one smiled and said, "I'm not so special really. I'm just like most other Stepkins. My name is Pidge."

Pidge explained that Stepkins are people, just as tall as a step, who live under the stairs.

"My brother Oggie and I were out picking wild blackberries for dinner, but we got lost. Then your dog decided to give me a ride in his mouth. Now I don't know where to find Oggie," said Pidge.

"I bet Moochie can find him," said Sadie. "Moochie, fetch!"

< 49 >

What can Sadie do to make herself feel happier?

< 50 >

So Moochie ran off and, sure enough, he returned in a few minutes with a wiggling and shouting Stepkin. It was Oggie.

Pidge introduced her brother, Oggie, who was carrying a whole sack full of wild berries.

"Are you picking blackberries, too?" asked Oggie.

"No," said Sadie. "I'm just wasting time with Moochie. No one else wants to spend time with me." She felt very sorry for herself.

"Well then, why don't you help us pick berries for supper. It's our job," said Pidge.

"Yes," said Oggie, "that might cheer you up. Helping out always makes us feel happier."

< 51 >

How can Sadie get twice as much love?

< 52 >

So Sadie started to work helping the Stepkins find more berries.

"Feeling better?" asked Pidge, popping berries into her basket.

"Well, I really shouldn't feel happy," said Sadie. "I think my dad must be very lonely now, because Mom got married again."

"I have a hunch," said Oggie, "the thing that will make your dad feel the best is for you to be happy yourself."

"But it's a lot harder to be happy now that Mom has a new husband to love," said Sadie.

Pidge reached for a berry just over her head. "When Moochie first came into your family, did you love your mom or dad any less?"

"Of course not," said Sadie, biting into a berry that was not quite ripe.

"In the same way, your mother doesn't love you any less because she has a new husband. Now she has twice as much love. You see, you get more love when you share it, not less," said Pidge.

< 53 >

Can Sadie care about both her dad and Rudy at the
same time?

< 54 >

Oggie had been making a snack out of a ripe blackberry, but he stopped nibbling long enough to say, "Maybe the reason you feel bad is because you haven't exactly been helping lately or doing your share to make your new family work."

Sadie looked down at the ground, remembering how terribly she had acted by ruining the wedding pictures.

"The best way you can show your love for your mom is by talking with her about your feelings. Treat your new stepfather just the way you would like him to treat you, with respect and courtesy. You can even have fun with him," said Oggie, licking a dribble of berry juice off his fingers.

"Actually," said Sadie, "he has been kind of nice to me. He even built Moochie a new doghouse all by himself. But, I still miss having my dad at home."

< 55 >

Why does Sadie feel better?

< 56 >

"Well, be sure to tell your dad that you're glad to be with him each time you're together," said Pidge. "That way, he'll know that you love him even though he isn't at home with you. You'll always be his daughter. You will miss him less if you can call him on the telephone, and write him letters, and draw pictures for him. No matter how far away he lives, your hearts can always be together."

That thought made Sadie feel a little better.

She smiled and said, "Let's finish picking these berries. I'll pick some for Auntie Peg, too."

It felt good helping out, and Sadie got so busy that she forgot to spend time worrying.

When Oggie and Pidge had picked all the berries they could carry, they said good-bye to Sadie.

"But how can I see you again?" asked Sadie.

"Oh, that's simple," said Pidge. "Just peek under your stairs. We'll be there."

< 57 >

Why did Sadie draw a picture of Moochie sitting in his doghouse with a smile on his face?

< 58 >

When Sadie returned home, Auntie Peg was very surprised and pleased with the berries. "I'll make a special pie with the berries and we'll have it for dessert tonight. You know, Mom and Rudy will be home by dinnertime."

"At last!" said Sadie.

Then she had an idea.

She ran to her room and got out some poster paper and her paint set. Very carefully, she painted a banner that read "WELCOME HOME, MOM."

She also drew a picture. It was of Moochie sitting in his new doghouse with a big smile on his face. Thinking about how happy Mom and Rudy would be to see the sign made Sadie feel good inside.

She was all ready to pin up her banner by the front door when she had another idea.

With her paintbrush, she changed the banner. Now it read "WELCOME HOME, MOM AND RUDY."

Sadie showed Moochie the banner and the picture. Moochie gave Sadie a big lick. Then Sadie smiled as she waited for Mom and Rudy to walk through the door. She had some big hugs waiting for both of them.

< 59 >

Stepkin
Holidays

How a child copes with some necessary changes when he acquires a stepparent.

< 61 >

Stepkin Holidays

Before beginning this story, see general instructions on page 1.

In this story, a young boy named Spencer Pepper exhibits several common reactions to his custodial mother's new husband. You may have observed some or all of these reactions in the child you are helping:

Retaliation: Children frequently try to sabotage a parent's relationship by acting out, regressing, or manipulating. Often they are still expressing anger about the initial divorce.

Authority Conflict: Children are normally reluctant to accept a new stepparent automatically as an authority figure. They will normally discount the authority of the stepparent.

Jealousy: Children often have very possessive feelings toward parents, especially those of the opposite sex. They sometimes perceive a parent's new spouse as a threat to their own relationship with the parent.

Anxiety about Life Style Changes: Any family habit becomes routine to a child. When a new stepfamily is formed, the many routine changes that normally occur are stressful for the child to cope with because he/she is not sure what to expect next.

Allegiance to the Absent Parent: Children may see a parent's remarriage as betrayal of the ex-spouse. Consequently, they feel guilty about showing affection toward the new stepparent and will show fierce loyalty to the absent parent.

< 62 >

Reading this story with the child will help him/her realize these feelings are normal with a new stepparent. If you discuss Spencer Pepper's problems and how he begins to cope with them, you can gradually begin to talk with the child about his or her own feelings and reactions.

Using your own words and examples, explain the following points to the child:

- The child is a participant in family activities and decisions.
- Children need to talk about their feelings and actively find ways to contribute to the family.
- The relationship with the new stepparent will not be the same as with the natural parent. One relationship need not diminish the other.
- The child needs to be courteous to new stepparents, although natural parents have primary responsibility for directions and guidance.
- Although the life style changes may be stressful, they also represent new opportunities.
- Showing affection toward the stepparent is not a betrayal of the absent parent.
- If an absent parent shows no interest in a child, it does not mean the child is bad.
- The child may contact or share cards and gifts with both parents and stepparents on holidays.
- If the child can't be with a parent, it helps to call and write.
- The child should not feel guilty for not feeling love for the stepparent right away.
- The child is expected to show respect and courtesy to the stepparent and can expect the same in return.

< 63 >

Why is this Christmas different for Spencer?

< 64 >

Spencer Pepper tried to look very pleased with the dictionary Mom gave him for Christmas. He tried even harder to act happy about the strange looking socks Aunt Nancy had sent him. But the gift he really liked the best was a big magnifying glass that made things look much bigger than they really were.

The problem was, his favorite gift was not from his favorite person. It was from his stepdad, Kyle.

For some reason, Spencer didn't want to show Kyle how much he really liked the magnifying glass. You see, this was Spencer's first Christmas with Kyle. They lived in a new home, and things just didn't seem normal.

For example, they celebrated Hanukkah with Kyle before Christmas, and Spencer had never done that before. And on Christmas morning, Kyle passed out all the Christmas gifts. Dad always used to let Spencer pass out the gifts.

So many things were different now. It made Spencer worry because he wasn't ever quite sure what would happen next. In fact, on Christmas Eve, Spencer had worried so much that he had the worst nightmare ever. He dreamed that Santa Claus didn't know Spencer had moved, so he gave Spencer's presents to the little girl who had moved into Spencer's old house. And in Spencer's dream, Kyle decided to take the Christmas tree down before Spencer even got out of bed on Christmas morning.

"What a nightmare!" thought Spencer when he woke up and realized it had only been a dream.

< 65 >

Why is Spencer angry?

< 66 >

Spencer had run downstairs as fast as he could to make sure the tree was still there. It was, and luckily Santa had somehow figured out where to find Spencer.

Even with presents, things hadn't gone the way Spencer hoped. He was waiting for a very special phone call, a phone call from his dad who had moved to another state. Spencer had mailed Dad a new picture of himself with a card he had made. But the call hadn't come on Christmas eve. And the call hadn't come on Christmas morning. Somehow that made Spencer both angry and sad at the same time. And for some reason, he thought the person he should be mad at was Kyle.

Instead of smiling and giving Kyle a hug when Spencer opened the gift from Kyle, Spencer had just mumbled, "Thanks. I think I'll go outside."

"How about first picking up the wrapping paper and ribbons?" said Kyle.

"Do I have to?" whined Spencer.

"Get busy, young man," answered Mom. "You can go outside afterward."

So Spencer made a face while he hurried and picked up the wrapping paper.

Why didn't the phone ring? he wondered.

He picked up the telephone and checked just to make sure it was still working.

When he found it was working fine, he slammed it down and stomped out of the house, taking his new magnifying glass with him.

< 67 >

Why does Spencer want to be by himself?

< 68 >

Outside, the cool air helped settle down Spencer's temper, and he began exploring with his magnifying glass.

He thought it would be interesting to look at some bugs with his glass, so he poked around the flower pots. But he couldn't seem to find any bugs, not a spider, not even a little ladybug.

Then Spencer decided to look around the front porch steps. Since they were made of wood, he thought he might be able to find some termites hiding in the cracks between the boards.

So Spencer crawled along the steps, with his magnifying glass, hoping at least to find an ant or two.

When Spencer came upon a big hole in one of the boards, he noticed a very strange thing. He thought he saw lights shining out from the hole.

But how could that be?

So he climbed very close and peeked through the hole with his magnifying glass. What he saw made him think he must be dreaming again. There were people under the stairs! Well, not exactly people, because they were only as tall as a step, and they had lovely twinkling lights just above their ears.

< 69 >

Should Spencer talk about how he feels?

< 70 >

The little people had a cozy home under the steps, decorated with bits and pieces of things they had found. Dancing and singing together, they seemed so happy that Spencer decided it was time to meet the little group.

He crawled to the side of the stairs and said, "Hello."

Hanging over the edge of the stairs with his magnifying glass, Spencer must have looked very strange. The little people stopped their dancing and singing and stared at Spencer hanging upside down.

"I'll be right down," Spencer said, and he scrambled as fast as he could to squeeze himself under the steps to join the little group. This was much better than looking for bugs.

He wanted to meet these little people and find out why they were so small. "I'm Spencer Pepper," he said. "I've moved in upstairs."

The smallest of the group seemed to be the bravest, and he spoke right up.

"I'm Tipper Stepkin. And this is my big sister, Posy. Come meet Mum and Pop. We've been celebrating the holidays with some singing and dancing. Would you like to join us?"

"Oh, I'll just watch," said Spencer.

< 71 >

How do adults show children they love them?

< 72 >

So Mum began playing her little banjo made from tossed-away rubber bands and a wooden ice-cream spoon, while Pop played his thimble and bottle cap drums. Tipper and Posy danced in a circle while they all sang together.

When they were done, Posy offered Spencer some of their special holiday Nut Nog to drink and said, "We're glad you moved in upstairs. Do you live with your family?"

"I wish I did," said Spencer, "but I live with my mom and my stepfather."

"That sounds like a family to me," said Pop.

"But I wish I could be with my real dad," said Spencer. "Christmas must be sad for him without me because he loves me so much."

Mum said, "Well, I'm sure your stepfather loves you too, Spencer."

Spencer scratched his head and thought for a moment. "I'm not really sure if he does or not."

"It's easy enough to tell," said Mum, pouring Spencer another tiny cup of Nut Nog. "Parents show their love by the things they do with their children. Does your stepfather help you when you're in trouble? Does he take care of you when you're sick or hurt?"

< 73 >

Why didn't Spencer want to give Kyle a hug?

< 74 >

Spencer thought back to when he had crashed on his bike. Kyle had carefully bandaged Spencer's knee and fixed the broken bicycle wheel. "Yes, I guess he does."

"And does he try to make time to spend with you? And does he act proud when you do something special?"

Spencer nodded yes, remembering how happy Kyle seemed with the pencil cup Spencer had made in school. Kyle filled it right up with pencils and set it on the very front of his desk where everyone could see.

"Those are the ways parents show their love for children," said Mum, putting her arms around Tipper and Posy.

"Well, Kyle tries to hug me sometimes," said Spencer. "But I think it might make my dad unhappy if he knew."

Pop looked up. He was making a little bowl from a walnut shell. He said, "You know, Spencer, a stepparent might be different than a natural parent, and they might love you in different ways. But the thing that will make both fathers feel the best is knowing you're happy and doing fine with the changes in your life."

"Just do happy things, and your feelings will follow," said Mum, putting away the pitcher of Nut Nog.

"Like hugging?" asked Spencer.

"Sure," said Pop. "Remember, the things that you do for another person will show your love."

Spencer remembered how crabby he acted at Mom and Kyle when they asked him to pick up the Christmas wrapping paper. He felt sorry about the way he had acted and decided it was time to do something about it.

< 75 >

How does Kyle feel when Spencer asks him to go hunting for bugs?

< 76 >

He said good-bye to the Stepkins and asked if he could come and visit them again.

"Of course," said Mum. "We'll be here whenever you need us. Good luck, Spencer."

Spencer went into the house and looked at the mess around the Christmas tree. He hadn't done a very good job of cleaning up, so he picked up all the tiny scraps of gift paper and torn ribbons he hadn't picked up the first time. And he put all the opened gifts neatly under the tree—Mother's new scarf and slippers, Kyle's new cologne and necktie, even Spencer's new dictionary and the funny looking socks from Aunt Nancy.

Kyle came in and saw how nice the room looked. "Hey, you did a good job, Spencer."

And Mom said, "Why don't you go out and play awhile before dinner. The turkey won't be done for a bit."

Spencer remembered what the Stepkins had told him, and he said to Kyle, "Do you want to look for bugs with my magnifying glass?"

"Sure. I haven't done that in a long time," said Kyle, and off they went in search of bugs.

Kyle showed Spencer how to turn over rocks to find bugs and worms.

They found a great little beetle that looked wonderful under the magnifying glass. Spencer named it Rocky, and Kyle helped Spencer put it into a jar and hammer breathing holes in the lid.

< 77 >

Why did Spencer want to give Kyle a hug?

< 78 >

"You can take Rocky to school for Show and Tell and let the other kids look at him through your magnifying glass. Then we'll put him back under his rock," said Kyle.

"I'd like that," said Spencer. Then, realizing what he meant to say, he added, "I really like the magnifying glass, too."

He gave Kyle a big hug to say thanks.

Kyle hugged Spencer back and said, "You've just given me a nice gift too, Spencer."

< 79 >

Jamie
and the
Stepkins

A story of a child dealing with a new sibling in a new stepfamily.

< 81 >

Jamie and the Stepkins

Before beginning this story, see general instructions on page 1.

In this story, a young boy named Jamie McNulty exhibits several common reactions to a stepsibling. You may have observed some or all of these reactions in the child you are helping:

Anger: The remarriage of a parent often destroys the child's fantasy that the natural parents will someday reconcile. The result is anger toward the natural parent, the new stepparent, and the new stepsibling(s).

Territoriality: Children have a strong sense of ownership about their belongings and their rooms. If a stepfamily requires a child to change or share these things, it can be quite distressing, causing the child to appear stubborn, possessive, or selfish.

Resistance to Change: When stepfamilies are formed, they normally combine different habits, rules, likes, and dislikes. For the child who has come to expect certain family routines, even minor changes can be highly stressful.

Reconciliation Fantasy: Children will not only often spend time fantasizing about natural parents remarrying, but they will sometimes feel their wishful thinking can actually make things change the way they would like.

Jealousy: Children often have very possessive feelings toward parents, especially those of the opposite sex. They sometimes perceive the parent's new spouse as a threat to their own relationship with the parent.

Guilt Feelings: Children frequently take the responsibility for the divorce on their own shoulders. They think if they had not acted badly, the divorce would not have happened. This sense of control also leads them to believe it is within their power to reconcile the parents and restore the marriage.

< 82 >

Reading this story to the child will help him/her realize these feelings are normal in a divorce and stepfamily situation. If you then discuss Jamie McNulty's problems and how he learns to cope with them, you can gradually begin to talk with the child about his or her own feelings and reactions to the stepfamily.

Using your own words and examples, explain the following points to the child:

- A parent's love for the child is no less because the parent remarries.
- Although the life style changes may be stressful, they also represent new opportunities.
- Children need to talk about their feelings and actively find ways to work things out.
- Everyone has both good points and bad points, and it is good to learn to be tolerant.
- If children begin behaving with happy and loving actions, even though they don't feel like it at first, their feelings may eventually improve.
- Establishing a relationship with the parent's new spouse is not a betrayal of the absent parent.
- Stepfamilies create new life style changes for all family members and require compromises by everyone.
- The child needs to talk about anger instead of running away or trying to hurt others. The anger may be caused by fear—and talking and hugging can help relieve the fear.
- It may help the child to talk about divorce with stepsiblings because they are going through similar experiences.

< 83 >

Why does Jamie feel unlucky?

< 84 >

Jamie McNulty was sure he was the unluckiest boy in the world.

It hadn't always been that way. When he was younger, things were better. He had his mom. He had his dad. They both took care of him in their house on Twenty-second Street. He even had his very own tree house Dad built for him in the backyard.

But then the terrible arguing started, and Dad left the house in a great big huff. Mom didn't stop crying for the longest time. Jamie began to learn about divorce.

For a long while, it was just Jamie and Mom. That is, until Rex and Ben came along.

Rex was the man who drove the school bus, and one day Rex and Mom got married.

"You have a new stepdad," Mom had said, "and a step-brother, Ben, as a bonus."

Jamie wanted to shout, "I want my own dad back! And if you love Rex and Ben, how can there be any love left for me?"

But he kept still because he loved Mom very much, and he wanted her to be happy.

"Give it a try, just for me," Mom had said. So he tried his hardest to like his new home life.

But one Saturday, when Ben came to stay for the weekend, Jamie became madder than he had ever been in his life.

< 85 >

Why did Jamie become so angry?

< 86 >

First of all, Jamie had to share his own bedroom with Ben, and Ben said he wanted to sleep on Jamie's top bunk bed. The top bunk was Jamie's favorite. Mom said Jamie should let Ben have his choice.

And worse, Ben borrowed Jamie's new kite without even asking and tore it on a tree branch.

And when Mom said, "Let's order pizza tonight," Ben said, "Can we have mushrooms on it?"

"Yuck!" Jamie said. "I hate mushrooms, and I won't eat them."

"That's too bad, young man," Mom said.

"That does it!" Jamie shouted.

He ran out the door, slamming it as hard as he could.

< 87 >

Why did Jamie pretend to run away from home?

< 88 >

Jamie hid in his tree house and frowned and made his hands into fists.

"If I run away, everyone will be sorry," thought Jamie. "I know, I'll just hide under the porch steps. I'll wait until it's late, so Mom will know what it's like when I'm missing. Then she will show everyone that she loves me the best, and maybe she'll call Dad to help find me."

So down Jamie crept to the porch steps to hide. He had always wondered what was underneath them.

He pulled back the boards to climb under, but suddenly he stopped. He felt something move under his fingers.

What could it be?

A snake?

Or a bug?

"Ouch!" something squeaked.

"Yikes!" Jamie shrieked. "Hey, a bug can't talk like a person."

"Who are you calling a bug?"

< 89 >

Who should Jamie talk to about his feelings?

< 90 >

Jamie whispered, "What are you then?"

"I'm not a what. I'm a who. And you gave me a fright."

"Well, you gave me one too, so we're even. I'm Jamie McNulty."

Something stepped into view that looked sort of like a little boy. He had freckles, like Jamie, and bright fudge-brown eyes. But, he was only as tall as a step. And more amazing yet, twinkling light came from the top of his curly-haired head.

"I'm Jessup Stepkin."

"Where did you come from?" asked Jamie.

"Right here," Jessup said. "We Stepkins live under your porch steps. We oil your steps every day so they won't squeak. Come and meet my family."

Jamie wiggled himself under the porch and found himself in the tiniest little home.

The darkness was lit by the beautiful glow from the Stepkins' twinkling lights.

With furniture made from tossed-away jars and cartons, the Stepkins had made a cozy home. The Stepkins were very clever with scraps. A tin can made a table. Cereal boxes were beds, and a comfy sponge made their sofa.

"How do you do?" said Ma Stepkin.

"Pleased to meet you," said Pa Stepkin.

Toby and Tot, the little Stepkin twins, just giggled and tumbled around the room.

The Stepkins were the friendliest people. They shared some clover juice in nutshell cups with Jamie.

< 91 >

Does Ben try to make Jamie angry on purpose?

< 92 >

"Can I hide in your home for a little while?" Jamie asked.

"Hide?" said Ma Stepkin. "Why, what's the matter?"

So Jamie explained his whole sad story, about Dad and Rex and Ben. "Ben broke my new kite, and I'm so mad. He caught it on a tree."

"I see," said Ma, nodding with a smile. Then she asked him, "Have you ever caught a kite on a tree?"

"Well, yes," said Jamie.

"And did you do it on purpose?" she asked.

"Well, no," said Jamie.

Ma poured Jamie some more clover juice from the old salt shaker she used as a pitcher.

"So don't you think it was also an accident when Ben broke your kite, Jamie?" asked Ma.

"But," Jamie said, "he also wants to sleep on the top of my bunk bed, and that's my place."

"My goodness, I would worry about falling off, if I were on the top bunk," said Ma Stepkin, picking up Toby who had squashed Tot on the floor. "Don't you think you could take turns with Ben sleeping on the top bunk?"

"Well, I guess so," said Jamie, "But why should I have to?"

"You don't have to," said Ma, "but every time you do something nice for Ben, like magic something nice will come back to you. Remember that Ben is learning how to be a stepbrother, just like you."

< 93 >

Was the divorce Jamie's fault?

< 94 >

"But," said Jamie, "none of this would have happened if Mom and Dad hadn't argued so much and Dad hadn't left home. It's all my fault."

"What did they argue about?" asked Pa.

"Oh, Dad did things that made Mom mad, and Mom did things that made Dad mad," said Jamie.

"How could it be your fault then, Jamie? A child cannot make parents leave each other," said Pa. "And what was it like when your mother and father were still married?"

"The shouting and crying hurt my feelings. I kept wishing things would be different," sighed Jamie.

"Aren't things different now?" asked Pa.

Ma sat down on her pin-cushion chair to work on the slippers she was knitting for Jessup.

"I guess Mom and Rex are happy together. But I wish it was like the old days, before Mom and Dad began fighting," said Jamie.

"We can't bring back the past," said Ma Stepkin, "but we can bundle up the happy memories and tuck them safely in our hearts. You can make new memories now, in your blended family."

< 95 >

How can Jamie help the family to get along better?

< 96 >

"I don't feel happy," said Jamie, "but I guess I can act like I am."

"That will work fine for now," said Ma. "If you act like you're happy long enough, your sad feelings will have a hard time sneaking out."

"But I don't love Rex and Ben like I love Mom and Dad," said Jamie.

"No need to for now," said Pa Stepkin. "Just treat them the way you would like them to treat you."

Jamie tried to hide the little tear that started to roll down his freckled nose. "But Mom won't love me the same if she loves them, too."

Ma Stepkin understood Jamie's worry. "The magic thing about love is that it never gets used up. Your mother doesn't love you less because she has Rex and Ben in the family. She has three times as much love now. How lucky she is! And you're a lucky boy too, Jamie."

< 97 >

Can Jamie's mother care about both Jamie and Ben at the same time?

< 98 >

Just then, the smell of pizza being delivered reached Jamie's nose, and he realized it was getting late. He said good-bye to the Stepkin family and promised to come back and visit them soon.

"Next time, why don't you bring Ben along?" invited Ma.

Jamie promised to think about it, and he crawled out from under the steps.

When he ran into the kitchen, Jamie's mother said, "Oh good, you're home just in time for pizza, Jamie."

And Ben said, "Look, Dad and I fixed your kite. It's almost as good as new. I'll be more careful next time."

"Thanks," said Jamie, acting a little bit happy. He even got part of his mouth to smile.

Jamie kept smiling while he ate his pizza, and he noticed that Ben and Mom and Rex started smiling too. And pretty soon, Jamie didn't have to pretend he was having a good time. He really did feel happy, just like Ma Stepkin had said.

< 99 >

Would Ben understand what it is like for a child's
parents to divorce?

< 100 >

After pizza, Rex helped the boys make a special project. They took a piece of garden hose and put a funnel on each end.

They put one end on the top bunk bed and one on the bottom. It made the best Secret Message Machine ever.

Snuggled in bed, the boys shared secret stories, talking through their Secret Message Machine.

As Jamie started to fall asleep, he said in a drowsy voice, "Good night, Ben. Be sure to get lots of rest for tomorrow—have I got something under the steps to show you!"

Then Jamie fell fast asleep, thinking about what a lucky day this had been.

< 101 >

Sailing
with the
Stepkins

A child learns to solve problems when visiting a noncustodial parent.

< 103 >

Sailing with the Stepkins

Before beginning this story, see general instructions on page 1.

In this story, a young girl named Emma Holliday exhibits several common reactions to being transferred back and forth between homes after her parents' divorce. You may have observed some or all of these reactions in the child you are helping:

Frustration: Children often have an image in their minds about how a family should be structured, usually based on their earliest experiences. If they are unable to restore this model, they become frustrated.

Trying to Fill in for the Lost Spouse: Girls will often try to fill the role of an absent mother, and boys will try to take the place of an absent father. They try to take on responsibilities which prove to be overwhelming and may not devote adequate time to their peer group.

Disappointment over Broken Commitments: When a child spends time going back and forth between divorced parents, the added scheduling complications and typical communication breakdowns make it difficult for parents to keep commitments to children. Children often take these disappointments personally, even if they are unavoidable.

Stress Reactions: Not only is the initial divorce stressful for children, but transferring between parents is also a strain. This is particularly true if parents use the children to communicate with the ex-spouse.

Anxiety over Life Style Changes: Any family habit becomes routine to children. When divorce changes many of these routines, children become anxious because they do not know exactly what they can expect.

< 104 >

Reading this story with the child will help him/her realize these feelings are normal when sharing time between divorced parents. If you discuss Emma Holliday's problems and how she begins to cope with them, you can gradually begin to talk with the child about his or her own feelings and reactions.

Using your own words and examples, explain the following points to the child:

- A child cannot take the place of a lost spouse.
- Even though the family has been reorganized, all family members must try their best to keep commitments.
- Children visiting a noncustodial parent should not be entertained constantly. It is important to spend time in normal family activities.
- A child should not be used as a go-between. The parents need to communicate directly with each other.
- Allegiance to one parent is not a betrayal of the other parent. A child should not be encouraged to choose sides.
- A child should not carry the burden of trying to make the divorced parents get along with each other.
- Children need to talk about their feelings and actively find ways to make things work.
- It is all right for the children to give hugs and kisses to the parents in front of each other, even though the parents are not hugging or kissing each other.
- The parents may make mistakes that they need to work out, without help from the child.
- Sometimes there will be less money available after the divorce and the child will need to adjust to different circumstances.
- The child should ask the parents for help in keeping track of schedules.

< 105 >

Why does Emma want to take care of her father?

< 106 >

Emma Holliday was having a terrible Saturday morning. She hoped that her visits to Daddy's new little apartment wouldn't all be like this.

The trouble started when she decided to try and fix breakfast for Daddy. Mom always used to cook Daddy's breakfast, but since the divorce, Emma worried about how Daddy would get his meals. He was not the best cook in the world.

So Emma decided to cook him a great breakfast all by herself. She had watched Mom so many times, she thought it would be a snap. But it was so hard to find the pots and pans in two different kitchens.

And the cooking did not go smoothly either. When she cracked the eggs, tiny pieces of the shells fell into the pan, and they were so slippery to try and pick up.

Then, when she tried to do the scrambling part, lumps of eggs jumped out of the pan and fell down into the hot burner. What a smelly, smoky mess they made!

Then the toast was a problem. The bread was a little too long for the slot in the toaster, so Emma smashed it down a bit. But then it was stuck and couldn't pop out when it was done. It just sat in the toaster and burned. Mom's toast never burned.

The hot cocoa didn't help her out much either. It looked downright scary and dribbled all the way from the sink to the stove. But when Daddy got up, he tried to act like he enjoyed breakfast—even the crunchy eggs.

< 107 >

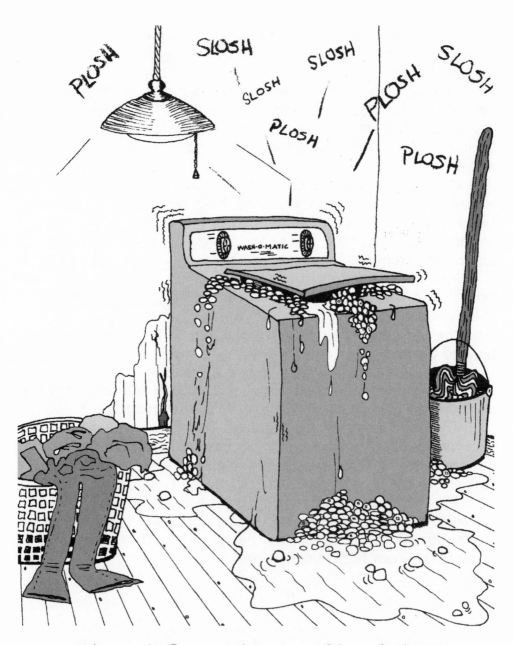

Why can't Emma take care of her father?

< 108 >

After breakfast, Emma decided to help Daddy by doing his laundry. So she picked up his brand new, bright red bathrobe, some muddy white socks, and all the white towels from the bathroom and stuffed them in the washing machine. Some nice hot water would get them clean, especially with the extra soap she added for those muddy socks.

Slosh, plosh. Slosh, plosh. Slosh, plosh. The washer began its job, so she went to look for some clothes to wear. It was so hard to remember where her clothes were in two different homes. Just as she was finishing putting on her shoes, she heard Daddy cry, "Oh, no!" from the laundry room.

Worried, Emma quickly ran to the laundry room. There was Daddy, standing in pink soap bubbles up to his knees.

"Uh oh," said Emma. "Guess I sort of goofed, huh?" She felt terrible.

"I know you were trying to help," said Daddy. "Well, let's get this mess cleaned up. Then how about going down to the park together?"

"Okay," said Emma, pulling the mop and bucket out of the broom closet.

When they were finished cleaning up, Daddy and Emma went down to the park, and Daddy found a nice shady spot under a tree. Before long, he was napping, so Emma decided to walk down to the little duck pond close by. As she got near the pond, she thought she heard some funny sounding birds. But it actually sounded more like tiny voices calling for help.

What could it be? she wondered. She pushed aside the tall grass growing at the edge of the pond, and there, standing before her eyes, was the most amazing sight.

< 109 >

Was Emma's father angry about the messes she made?

< 110 >

Two little creatures were floating on a small raft made of twigs. Beautiful twinkling lights glowed just above their ears.

The raft had a dandy sail made from a big maple leaf, but it was caught on some rocks and was stuck out in the pond.

The raft wouldn't move. When the little people noticed Emma, they stopped their shouting, and one of them said, "Oh, you're so big. Can't you please help us? We've been stuck here for the longest time."

Emma smiled and said, "Sure, I'd be glad to help."

She took off her shoes and socks, rolled up her pant-legs, and waded into the pond until she could reach the raft. She carefully untangled it from the rocks and pushed it safely to shore.

< 111 >

What can Emma do to help her father?

< 112 >

So happy to be back on land, the two little ones jumped around and hugged each other and said, "Oh thank you, thank you so much."

Then they introduced themselves to Emma. Their names were Nubbin and Dot Stepkin.

"We live under the steps at the library," said Nubbin.

Then Emma understood why they were only as tall as a step.

"We thought we were pretty good sailors," said Nubbin. "But we didn't do such a great job today."

"I know how you feel," said Emma. "I've been messing things up all day."

"What did you do?" asked Nubbin, tying the raft to a big cattail.

"Well, I wanted to do all the things Mom did for Daddy when they used to be married," said Emma.

"But Emma," said Dot, "a child cannot take care of a parent. That's too big a job."

< 113 >

Should it be Emma's job to take messages between her parents?

< 114 >

"But my daddy really needs me," Emma said, sitting down at the edge of the pond. "He seems so sad whenever I'm supposed to come visit him and Mom changes her mind about letting me come."

"Well, of course," said Nubbin, "whenever we plan on something special, we are sad if it doesn't happen."

"I guess that's why Mom gets so worried when Daddy brings me home late," said Emma.

"That's right," said Nubbin, trying to catch a little water skipper who flew past his nose. "Even though your family has changed now, it's still very important for everyone to keep promises."

"Yes," said Dot. "You need to tell your parents it's important that you know what to expect. You need to tell your parents about how you feel, especially when something is troubling you."

"Well, one thing is bothering me," said Emma, wiggling her toes around in the pond. "Sometimes they ask me so many questions about what the other one is doing, I start to feel like a spy."

"Then the best thing for you to do," said Nubbin, "is just tell them you would like them to ask the questions directly to each other."

Dot added, "That way you won't have to worry about getting messages mixed up or hurting anyone's feelings."

"I'll try it tonight," said Emma, smiling.

Feeling much better, she helped Nubbin and Dot onto their raft and whirled them around in the water.

"Wheee," they squealed with delight. "Emma, this is fun!"

< 115 >

What kind of activities can Emma and her father plan together?

< 116 >

Before long, Emma heard Daddy calling her, so she had to say goodbye to the Stepkins.

"Can we play again?" she asked.

"Sure," said Dot, "We're always here on sunny days."

"I'll try to come again next Saturday," said Emma, and off she ran to meet Daddy.

When Daddy saw Emma, he said, "Ready for lunch?"

Emma was very hungry, but she didn't want to face the kitchen alone again, so she said, "Can we stop at the hot dog stand in the park?"

"Sounds like a good idea," said Daddy. "Come on."

After a lunch of hot dogs and lemonade, Emma and Daddy went back to his apartment.

"Shall we go to a movie this afternoon?" he asked.

But Emma felt like simply relaxing together, so she decided to tell Daddy how she felt. "Don't worry about keeping me busy all the time, Daddy. I'd be just as happy staying here."

"Well, I don't want you to get bored in this small apartment," said Daddy.

"I won't," Emma said. "It's fun just being together."

< 117 >

What can Emma do to help make sure she gets home on time?

< 118 >

So Emma climbed on one end of the sofa and read a book about dinosaurs, and Daddy relaxed on the other end with a book about business. While they read, they munched on popcorn that Daddy made all by himself.

Later, Emma helped Daddy fold his laundry. Daddy didn't complain when he saw that his new red robe had turned all of his white laundry pink because Emma had washed them together in hot water.

At dinner time she helped by setting the table and letting Daddy do the cooking. He didn't do badly at all.

"Daddy, I didn't know you could cook spaghetti," said Emma.

During dinner, Daddy asked some questions about Mom. Emma smiled and said, "Mom can tell you what she's been up to when you take me home. That way, I won't get any information mixed up." She winked at Daddy.

When it was time for Emma to go home to Mom's house, she told Daddy, "We better get going so we're not late."

Emma remembered the last time Daddy brought her home late. Mom was upset and said Daddy had done it on purpose.

"Being on time is keeping our word," Emma added.

Daddy smiled and said, "Let's get going then, Sweetheart."

So off they drove, singing songs along with the car radio. Emma decided that as soon as she got home, she would let Mom see her give Daddy a hug and kiss good-bye and let Daddy see her give Mom a hug and kiss hello.

This hadn't been such a bad Saturday after all. But a lot had happened, and Emma was ready to get back where Mom would be waiting to tuck her in bed.

< 119 >

Stepkin Summer

How a child learns to adapt to the challenges of visiting a noncustodial stepfamily.

< 121 >

Stepkin Summer

Before beginning this story, see general instructions on page 1.

In this story, a young boy named Radley Peebles exhibits several common reactions while visiting his father's new family. You may have observed some or all of these reactions in the child you are helping:

Stress Reactions: Not only is the initial divorce stressful for children, but transferring authority back and forth between parents is also a strain. This is particularly true if parents use the children to communicate with the ex-spouse.

Anxiety over Lifestyle Changes: Any family habit becomes routine to children. When divorce changes many of these routines, children become anxious because they do not know exactly what they can expect.

Jealousy: Children often have very possessive feelings toward their parents, especially those of the opposite sex. They sometimes perceive a parent's new spouse as a threat to their own relationship with the parent.

Authority Conflict: Children are normally reluctant to accept a new stepparent automatically as an authority figure. They will normally discount the authority of the stepparent.

Withdrawal: The common stress reaction of seeking isolation is a form of avoidance. In stepfamilies, children may resist joining in family activities, preferring to remain alone rather than deal with a situation about which they are unsure.

< 122 >

Reading this story with the child will help him/her realize these feelings are normal when visiting a stepfamily. If you then discuss Radley Peebles's problems and how he begins to cope with them, you can gradually begin to talk with the child about his or her own feelings and reactions.

Using your own words and examples, explain the following points to the child:

- Children need to talk about their feelings and actively find ways to make things work.
- Everyone has both good points and bad points, and it is good to learn how to be tolerant.
- Each child needs to participate in important family activities and decisions.
- Even though divorce has separated the original family, all family members should try their best to keep commitments.
- Although the lifestyle changes may be stressful, they also represent new opportunities which may be better than before.
- Establishing a relationship with a stepparent is not betrayal of the absent parent.
- If children begin behaving with happy and loving actions, even if they don't feel like it at first, their feelings may eventually improve.
- The relationship with the new stepparent will not be the same as with the absent parent. One relationship need not diminish the other.
- Parents show their love and caring by the things they do for the other family members.
- The child is expected to show respect and courtesy for the stepfamily members and can expect the same in return.
- The co-parents should have a special place for children to have their own things at each home.
- The child can only change his or her own behavior, not the behavior of others.
- Basic behavior rules must be followed at both homes, although there may be differences.

< 123 >

Why are the rules and habits at Radley's dad's house different than at his mom's house?

< 124 >

Radley Peebles couldn't feel less at home if he were on the moon.

It would have been fine visiting Dad for the summer, except it meant being away from his dog, Rowdy, and living with his new stepfamily, too. Dad had a new wife, Bridie, who wasn't really so bad. But she had a son of her own named Sherman, who Radley thought was a pain in the neck.

Radley had to share Sherman's bedroom, which was always in a terrible mess. Besides, Sherman was a bossy little boy who made it clear he was not pleased that Radley had invaded his room.

Radley didn't know if he could take a whole summer of this. They did things so differently here. For example, they came to breakfast in their pajamas and bathrobes. At home, Radley and Mom always got dressed before breakfast. And they let their cat, Gyro, climb on the furniture. At home, Rowdy could never ever climb on the furniture.

They didn't even eat the same food Radley was used to. One night at dinner, there was something new to Radley on his plate. He tried to cut it, but it was too tough. So he just poked it with his fork and tried to bite into it.

< 125 >

Why does Radley feel sick?

< 126 >

"Ouch," he cried when something sharp hurt his tongue.

Everyone looked up from dinner and started to laugh at poor Radley.

Sherman said jokingly, "Don't you even know what you're doing?" He pretended to bite into the funny green thing on his own plate. He said, "Ooh, ow, ouch, yeow!" making fun of Radley.

"It's not my fault," said Radley angrily. "My mother never makes me eat these green flowers for dinner."

"Now, boys," said Bridie. "This isn't a green flower, Radley. It is a vegetable called artichoke, and I'll show you how to eat it."

But Radley said, "My stomach hurts. May I be excused?"

"I'll get you some medicine," said Bridie.

She gave Radley some pink liquid that didn't taste too bad. Then she said, "I hope this will make you feel better soon," and she tried to give him a hug.

But Radley pulled away and said, "Can I go lie down?"

"Of course," she said.

So Radley went to the boys' bedroom to be alone while everyone else was eating dinner.

In the room, Radley opened his suitcase and took out his special box. It was just a cardboard box, but it had very important things in it: pictures of Mom and Dad and his dog Rowdy, the patch he earned at swimming class, the crystal clear shooter from his marble collection, an Army whistle, and two quarters left over from his allowance.

He didn't like the idea of Sherman snooping through his stuff. There really wasn't any safe place he could hide it in Sherman's messy bedroom, so he decided to go looking for a safe hiding place.

< 127 >

Why does Radley feel lonely?

< 128 >

Radley had a hunch the most private place to keep his box might be in the basement because no one seemed to go down there much. So he opened the basement door, turned on the light, and went down the stairs.

It was quite messy in the basement, with Dad's tools, some old furniture, and dusty old sports equipment.

He looked all around and spotted just the right place to hide his box underneath the stairs. But there was a big stack of boxes blocking his way, so he started to move them aside, one by one. Some boxes were quite heavy. Finally, when there was just one big box left to move, Radley thought he heard small voices.

This seemed strange because Radley thought he was alone downstairs. He slowly peeked over the big box, and his eyes lit up brightly when he saw where the sound was coming from.

< 129 >

How can Radley feel more at home with Bridie and Sherman?

< 130 >

There were two little people, no taller than a step, with beautiful twinkling lights coming from just above their ears. It looked as though they were playing some kind of game, because one of them had a blindfold on and was spinning around saying,

"Step tag, step tag,
Whatever you do,
Step tag, step tag,
I'll find you."

Then the other one said,

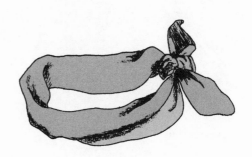

"Step tag, step tag,
Where can I be?
Step tag, step tag,
You can't find me!"

And then he took a big step—big for him, that is—away from the one with the blindfold.

Then the one with the blindfold tried to touch him while keeping one foot in place.

Radley thought this looked like a fun game, and he wanted to find out who these little people were anyway.

So, in a soft voice that wouldn't scare them, he said, "Hi. Can I play too?"

< 131 >

Should Radley talk about how he feels?

< 132 >

"Who was that?" said the little blindfolded one as she uncovered her eyes.

"My name is Radley Peebles."

"I'm Caprice Stepkin," said the one with the blindfold, "And this is my brother, Dooney."

"Do you live here?" asked Radley.

"We sure do," said Caprice. "Who do you think keeps the stairs from squeaking?" Then she asked, "Do you live here now too?"

"Not exactly," said Radley, climbing over the big box. "Usually I live with my mom, but this summer I'm living here with my dad and his new family."

"Aren't they your new family too?" asked Caprice.

"I don't know," said Radley. "I just feel like I don't belong here. They laugh at me and do things I'm not used to. And my stomach hurts a lot around here."

"We'll give you some Sparkling Stepkin Syrup to make your tummy feel better in no time." said Dooney.

< 133 >

How does Radley feel about Bridie and Sherman?

< 134 >

"That's okay," said Radley. "My stomach feels better now."

"Maybe that's because you talked about your feelings, Radley. It's very important to talk about how you're feeling with all these family changes," said Caprice. "And remember, the only way to discover good things is to go through changes sometimes."

"But sometimes Sherman laughs at me or makes fun of me," said Radley, "and it really makes me mad."

"Radley, you can decide whether you get mad or whether you laugh with Sherman," said Dooney. "It's always your choice, no one else's."

"I know Dad wants us all to get along, but there are just some things about Bridie and Sherman I don't like," said Radley.

"Well, that's normal," said Caprice, taking off her blindfold. "Everyone has both good points and bad points."

"But Bridie and Sherman don't feel like my family," said Radley.

"That's normal, Radley, because this family change is still new to you. It will take some time," said Dooney.

"You keep saying it's normal. But a normal family doesn't get divorced," said Radley.

"Oh, Radley," said Caprice, "every family is different, and there is no kind of family that is wrong. Lots of kids have families just like yours, and lots of kids have families that are different from yours. Any family can be happier if everyone tries their best."

< 135 >

What can Radley do to make himself feel better?

< 136 >

"But I feel so lonely when Dad spends time with Bridie and Sherman."

"You have a new kind of family now," said Caprice. "And maybe it would help if you started learning to do new things together, like teaching each other new things, helping each other with jobs, or playing games."

"And remember, Radley," added Dooney, "a child cannot decide who will be in his family. But you can make the choice whether you want to cause problems or try to help fix problems. When you help the others in your family, you help yourself."

"I guess I could try," said Radley.

"Good. Just give others exactly what you want to get back. Why don't you go give it a try then and let us know how it goes?" said Caprice.

"I will," promised Radley.

Radley said good-bye to the Stepkins, and then he took his special box back upstairs, thinking about what the Stepkins had said to him.

< 137 >

How does Bridie show that she cares about Radley?

< 138 >

Radley put his special box back in his suitcase, and then he went into the kitchen.

"I'm feeling better now," he announced to the family.

"That's wonderful," said Bridie, smiling. "How about some chocolate chip ice cream? I bought some especially because your dad said it was your favorite."

Chocolate chip ice cream! Radley and Dad always used to eat it together.

Bridie scooped out a dish for everyone, and afterward they all helped with the dishes. Dad cleared the table. Sherman washed the dishes. Radley dried them, and Bridie put them in the cupboard.

"Hey, the work goes quickly when everyone pitches in," said Dad. "We're a good working team. What shall we do this evening?"

Then Radley said shyly, "Would anyone like to learn to play Step Tag?"

To Radley's surprise, they all said they would like to play.

< 139 >

Can Radley care about Bridie and his mother at the
same time?

< 140 >

Bridie was the first with the blindfold. They spun her around and each took one giant step away in different directions. Then Radley told Bridie to say,

"Step tag, step tag,
Whatever you do,
Step tag, step tag,
I'll find you!"

Then Radley said back to her,

"Step tag, step tag,
Where can I be,
Step tag, step tag,
You can't find me."

Then Dad and Sherman copied him. They all stood perfectly still while Bridie tried to touch one of them while she kept one foot in place.

Bridie tried and tried, but she wasn't doing very well at catching anyone.

Suddenly, she said, "Gotcha, Radley!"

Dad and the boys laughed and laughed. Bridie took off her blindfold. What she had grabbed was Radley's jacket hanging on a coat rack.

Bridie was a good sport and began laughing with everyone. Radley thought it was nice when Dad went over and gave Bridie a great big hug.

Next it was Radley's turn for the blindfold, and he was going to be a good sport too.

As Sherman started to spin him around, Radley thought to himself, "Maybe this won't be such a horrible summer after all."

< 141 >

To order additional copies of

The Stepkin Stories

Book: $16.95   Shipping/Handling: $3.50

Contact: ***BookPartners, Inc.***
P.O. Box 922, Wilsonville, OR 97070
Fax: 503-682-8684
Phone: 503-682-9821
Phone: 1-800-895-7323